Days into Flatspin

ALSO BY KEN BABSTOCK

Mean

Ken Babstock

Days into Flatspin

Poems

Published in Canada in 2001 and in the United States in 2002 by
House of Anansi Press Limited
895 Don Mills Rd., 400-2 Park Centre
Toronto, ON M3C 1W3
Tel. (416) 445-3333
Fax (416) 445-5967
www.anansi.ca

Distributed in Canada by
General Distribution Services Ltd.
325 Humber College Blvd.
Etobicoke, ON M9W 7C3
Tel. (416) 213-1919
Fax (416) 213-1917
E-mail cservice@genpub.com

Distributed in the United States by
General Distribution Services Inc.
PMB 128, 4500 Witmer Industrial Estates
Niagara Falls, NY 14305-1386
Toll Free Tel. 1-800-805-1083
Toll Free Fax 1-800-481-6207
E-mail gdsinc@genpub.com

05 04 03 02   2 3 4 5

CANADIAN CATALOGUING IN PUBLICATION DATA

Babstock, Ken, 1970–
Days into Flatspin

Poems.
ISBN 0-88784-658-0

I. Title.

PS8553.A245D39 2001   C811'.54   C00-933192-1
PR9199.3.B32D39 2001

Cover design: Angel Guerra
Typesetting: Brian Panhuyzen
Printed and bound in Canada

THE CANADA COUNCIL | LE CONSEIL DES ARTS
FOR THE ARTS | DU CANADA
SINCE 1957 | DEPUIS 1957

*We acknowledge for their financial support of our publishing program the Canada
Council for the Arts, the Ontario Arts Council, and the Government of Canada
through the Book Publishing Industry Development Program (BPIDP).*

Barb Panter

and my brothers, Gavin, Peter, and Jason Babstock

Contents

Lords of the discontinuous, lords of the little gestures,
Succor my shift and save me . . .
— Charles Wright

Prologue

Then *Not much of anything at all. Not much.*

Less. Then *Pine needles, lion-coloured,*
withering on the dormer's shingle.

Then *The sad surcease of whatever*
sound track had up until then been playing.

Then *A rocket, piercing the up-there becomes many. Writes*
onto the sky the sky's eulogy. A fountain. Toss a coin in.

Then *"Get the hell out of that pear tree!"*

Then *Narrative. My reasons are good for showing you this. It unfolds.*

Then *Strung together like the bored but devout, a few*
notes. O upward tug, a few notes. Unfolding.

Then *A thing. Shall we name it?*
This could get tricky.

Then *For all that, we remain.*

Then *Remain. Anything at all.*

Carrying someone else's infant past a cow
in a field near Marmora, Ont.

Summer gnats colonized her molasses black eyes, her flicking,
conical ears. She moaned, a badly tuned
tuba, and tassels of ick dripped
from her black-

on-pink nostrils like strings of weed sap. Waking from a rhythmic
nap in my arm, you wobbled your head upright
and stared at the great hanging skin-
bag, teats, dry-docked

hull of her ribs, anvil head, and the chocolate calm in her eyes
that gazed back as I carried you closer, wading
through goldenrod, mulleins, thistle
all artfully bent

clear of your soft exposed feet. Ants worried the punky
tops of knotted fence posts, and caution flags
of gossamer and milkweed fluff
marked each rust-twist

of barb, but that was all that divided you and her. I felt briefly
happy to be prop, peripheral in this exchange,
this unfolding bundle of knowing that
was you in

an overgrown ditch where the air swelled, shaking itself dry
in the sumac. What was I shown that I haven't retained?
What peered back long before the cracked
bell of its name

came sounding off a tongue's hammer and fenced it forever? Know
that it happened, though — you were a drooling lump
of living in the verdant riddle. That heifer
remembers

nothing of you. Let chicory, later in life, be bothersome blue
asterisks footnoting one empty, unrecoverable
hour of your early and
strange.

Bottled Rabbit

A dream: of a stand of pole birch straight ahead
that drink into their moon-white trunks what little
light there is, then pose in stark relief to the darkening

beyond. The silence, though, is too complete, not right,
nothing shifts, whistles, or scuttles through the mess
of undergrowth. The effect, not of waking in the midst

of dark woods, the right road lost but the wringing
of phantom hands, a poverty of words, as the mind tries
to flush some authentic response to this charcoal study

by Cézanne. When waking comes it's to radio voices, a he
and a she, on about slips, snares, the gutting shed, and mason
jars. It's the CBC, in a town I didn't catch near Gander, doing

a segment, it seems, on the unusual folk dishes and dietary
habits of the ever-colourful Newfoundlander. ". . .bottled rabbit,"
he's saying, "today I'll show you how to make bottled rabbit, or

jarred rabbit, as it's called in other parts." And as the host
gives a slowed-down translation that imparts a tut-tut sound
to all the *t*'s, I'm seeing that reticent, cardiganed man in

the one-act by Pinter hauling up tiny masts on a glassed-in
schooner; only it's a matchstick bunny now, and he's trying to
attach the whiskers. "You can see I've already skinned, cleaned,

and quartered this one" (the whiskers quiver, fall off, the ears
lie back. The man sighs, lights up, starts in again) "and normally one
rabbit, quartered, 'll fit into each mason jar." It's here the Pinter

set fades, morphs, becomes my great-aunt's kitchenette twenty
years ago; the margarine-coloured curtains are closed, so
the light takes on a clinical, formaldehyde glow, and two jars

are eased down from a shelved row of preserved I-didn't-know-whats. A lid twists, its wax and rubber seal breaks with a sucking sound, bits of white fatty pulp drop from the lip and she dunks

two fingers and thumb through the film for the pink-brown, naked oblongs of meat. Perhaps we are what we remember we ate, but I've no memory, now, of what that rabbit tasted like, though I'm

tempted to say it tasted like rabbit. The host, here, pipes in unbelievably with "Wow, it tastes like chicken . . ." And thusly a nation is born, I thought, or something fuzzier that meant

that, as I was still barely awake. But you were coming to, just then, as they descended into clangorous cleanup noises, his water audibly bubbling in the pan. I touched your forehead: "What's real?"

Our aloe plant teetered on its chopstick struts, leaned over its double crawling the bedcover. The word wore down, thinned to a film on the air in the ear. Morning ate its hinge.

Flat

The front left this time, like a black
Dali clock, a cooling puddle of lava,
complete with its own vicious hiss.
We're caught, lame, on some sun-pounded

off-ramp or interchange; no jack, but
a perfectly usable, full-of-itself spare
in back offering all the insight and
aid of a thought-bubble inked in.

We hover, curse, kick the other three
as if this were their doing and listen to
that hiss-become-sigh from a World of
Things that has tired — not of its Being,

but of us. Hear it wishing, wishing
we'd either prepare ourselves fully
or leave off, stay home — or better,
be borne like a virus on the thickening air.

A Free Translation of Hardy's Darkling Thrush

This park gate's a stone arch
   quarried from pits. The pit's
now grown over and become another
   park, with the crane's legs of swings
and a skateboarder's painted bowl sunk in.
   I hang here, near a bronze
plaque fronting a monument to Hungary
   '56: a potted

shrapnel plant, memory's jagged
   isosceles welded to air.
Cellophane wrappers snag on power lines
   cross-hatching the sky. Starlings
like blips on a radar grid. No one
   comes. I invent an old guy,
humming Bartók, ambling up his front
   walk in the cribbage boards

of stiff brogues, cane punching divots
   in the mud verge. Seepage.
Fob watch. There's nowhere to be,
   so the chit-chitting of a grey
squirrel above me unhinges the hour and I open,
   flower, sure that he, or one like
him, has always been here. Which is which
   might not matter. Why

might not matter. He quivers in the naked
   aspen branches, balks,
our weather shudders through. Spruce
   cones, skinned twigs, the brittled
leaf-boats go calypso in time with his neurotic
   teeth. Worried hoardings.
Small percent of what gets stashed
   he'll later find.

Bear 10

Between next year's Lexus and someone
cooing at conditioner
he rakes his massive back along low spruce boughs.

How many pounds of Alaska berries in a day?
Smell it: dark, fecal
timbits steaming on flattened fireweed; the puffy,

antique dust-scent of pawed stump; dripping
cedar and glacier water
he laps at then glares into your living room, a barrel

of head rusted to distaste at what you've done
with the furniture. Harsh
light over the recliner and you *like* Kandinsky?

He's on a treadmill of alpine scenery from the west
half of the park to the Cariboo
range, this area filled in with a red matching the "on" indicator

blipping from his collar. Mike's picked up his transmission —
always Mike, or Walt — and they
know for a fact he's crashing this ridge unspooling into

the wherever beyond the framed glass of the chopper's cockpit.
— Seles in straight sets —
He's shovelling steelhead out of the frigid shallows,

mopping up a tributary of the Fraser that blackens him
to his throat. Hooks a nose
into a down-valley draft from offscreen. Single male

in a how many square kilometre tract? 10 likes his space.
— Everybody in khaki, Valvoline, Once
you pop you can't stop — but Mike has landed the bird

safely and shows us the overpass built for 10 and
they don't know if he's used it
but it appears well-engineered so why not. Could be

he's lumbering around the dank lee of the bookshelf
waiting to cross over in private,
chewing into the root-mat, a backhoe with breath, rolling

blowdown for the white nodes of grubs, hefting
his tonnage upright, wobbling
like a toddler for days through the wild grid looking

for nightfall and a back to embrace that won't break.

The 7-Eleven Formerly Known as Rx

Back in the day, I was proud of my vast palette
of candies; those for a penny over the front
counter, for kids and grannies, and the more
potent display locked in the back cabinet,

only ever given away if you'd come with a note
declaring you blocked, arthritic, headachy
or just couldn't say what was wrong for the frog
in your throat. Now, I sell mouthfuls of salt

to the stoned. It was snug in here, I was kept
stocked and swept by a family of five from Lisbon.
Now I'm grudgingly manned by tattooed kids
in green tunics helping themselves to the porn. And

the light in me's a perpetual migraine, I'm a super-
nova on a quiet corner, beacon to that fleet
of 4Runners and Acuras disgorging their thunder
of hip hop and jungle. I haven't slept since 1983.

To make space for the flavoured coffee station and
an ATM, they knocked out my east wall, expanded
onto the ribbon of lawn — not at all what that Aussie
meant when he defined "sprawl." I used to dream

in flamenco played on a push-button tape deck, or
the gurgle of talk radio on a Saturday, but I'm
lobotomized now, a drooler, listening to the Freon
drone from the dairy and drinks cooler. Gone

the licorice whips, manila envelopes, shampoo,
shaving kits; I'm all Scratch'n Win, *Vanity Fair*,
shellacked fruit, and the crinkling bladders of months-old
chips. I squat in my numbness and stare, recording

each night's parade of freaks on hidden surveillance
film. I'm hyperaware. I've begun to loathe
the intervals between guns when I have to convince
myself I'm still here. Oh, Maria, shelving hockey

cards while muttering lines by Pessoa; Papa's spirals
of suds greasing the glassfront; the boy out back
whacking tennis balls off my brick hip as the day
falls away. We stayed in the black but that

wasn't enough, nor was attaching Rx to the family name.
Atlanta home office faxes directives re: New Promo,
end aisle-ing my insides. They demand perfect rhyme: "I"
ground down, cauterized, shelved in the back of "franchise."

Anorak

It sounds like affliction, crisis, a medical condition;
something congenital between angina and heart
attack — definitely pulmonary/cardiac, and having
to do with clogs, unwanted buildup, congestion.

First sported by ice-eyed Norse and stitched
from the skins of luckless Celts or Picts, it fell out
of fashion for centuries, sharing that trunk
in the attic of ages with togas, lead-based cosmetics, the flayed

armadillos of chain mail and breastplate,
matching mastodon-fur slippers and robe. It's staged
a comeback though, shaken the webs
from its hollow head and burst from the closet.

A crack anti–air assault squad deployed
in a zip at the first volley of hail. It's hanging
in readiness from a hook on the wall above
our communal pile of polypropylene longjohns, splayed

bleached-out octopi lending our room
a Mediterranean look in midwinter, whiff of rosemary
like a seaport breeze, till I'm half-convinced I'm Ovid in snow
with a wicked jacket, transcending the hinterland's gloom,

incredulous in the storm of things changing form. As
though I'd ransacked, maybe, that trunk in the attic
and come down under one of those spiked, exclamatory lids
from the Kaiser's army: an echoing tin bowl of iffy ideas.

Boot Mat (After Géricault's *Raft of the Medusa*)

Never said *Welcome* but *Leave it at the door.*
Panning through slush for gravel, it was two square
feet of floating drama:

marbled Kodiacs, their scarred steel-toes tucked under
rad coils. The countable ribs of an emaciated galosh.
Perishing woolen mitt,

half on, half off; its sodden idiot string trailing
in the drink. A cold-blooded thing, it eked out a living
in the subarctic of the mud room.

We'd de-boot and set each out — winter's weepy
survivors — on this raft masted with the handles of shovels,
rigged with frayed scarves,

pass-me-down pullovers, and thrown on a meltwater swell.
It was that way. What's gone is art. Blessèd
galleon of the wood stove,

a brushed blip in the distance.

Tractor

Like mill wheels through a dark current, its herringbone
treads paddled through clumped earth and stone,

tossing pressed clots of brown dirt off their
upswing to fall, then, and remingle, aerated.

The small hinged cap atop a burping exhaust pipe
flapped in slow panic like the mother killdeer who'd taken a clip

from the tiller blade's edge for playing the martyr:
watched her furrowed nest of three eggs ploughed under

yet kept up her act while the flared cobra hoods
of the hammered rear-fenders cast shadows over sunned clods.

The valentine of the bucket seat perched on spring-coil: a metal palm-
leaf saddle burnished to a beach stone's gleam

that said a scooped-out I love you to any-sized ass.
A grumbling muscle, the grey bowels would hiss

and steam tendrils of mist if a sun shower passed over,
otherwise content, compressed in a throaty, subsurface worksong or

hymn that rattled its tin and heated the field's own dizzying heat.
I seemed to live on the thing when not in the bunkhouse, flat out,

dreaming spindly, front-axle dreams of the earth's intractable
turning under bloated, gear-cog tires that stood still

as they spun. We learned to be emptied, to become pure
function that summer. Dragged, reversing into row after row, acre

upon acre, until distance accordioned, time folded,
moments, hours became interchangeable dead

space our labour languished inside of. Drawing
figure eights with the gleaming hoes we hunched over, avoiding

green seedlings that appeared every other second or so
like metronomic ticks pacing our breathing, becoming a flow

we sat and worked in and ignored, spitting. Our necks gathered sun,
tightened, itched. Not four people pulled on the implement but one,

one, one, and one. Cowed into silence by the Go-Down-Moses,
near-nirvana breadth and bent grind of each day. An aching gnosis

punctuated by deerfly bites or an arm's numbed buzz when
a hoe rang the deep bell of a dislodgeable stone. We had fun,

alone together, dredging up privately what it was like to be elsewhere:
a moored midlake raft, drugged in a rec room, or almost untenable under

upright acres of mirrored glass, in a seed row of streetlight.

Fashion Consultant

That shirt! You're halfway there, lifted
out from the not-yet-thought-of and headed
for the burned-in-memory: ours and therefore
also yours. It's crisp and creased, squares

your shoulders, adds an inch to your back's
width, and where it enters those slacks
it dives in silently; that Olympic, spashless plop
that draws applause, perfect scores. Stop,

admit you beat doubt fair and square this morning
when, facing your twin, clad in that, you buttoned
up and couldn't argue a word against the feeling
you were more than theoretically there, outlined

in Japanese brush strokes, you were more than you;
perceptibly displaced the air while loosening the screw
of your neck to perform that *Exorcist* child-star
thing checking the tag's authenticity, like the pinch

the lucky talk about but never really do. And just to clinch
this experiment, make it watertight, even publishable —
I'll admit here's where my own baggage enters into it —
I'd like to watch you watching it where it leans awhile

in a stiff wind, pegged at its wrists and nape
to a creaking clothesline that spins on its pole
giving that shirt a recurring view of parted drapes
in a window where I'm reflected, and beyond

that complication can be made out a chilled, half-formed
figure we'll provisionally refer to as "you."

Sleeping on an Incline

"If [O'Brien] had any doubts about the faith in which he was brought up, they were on Manichaean grounds; somehow perhaps the balance of good and evil in the universe as we know it had been disturbed in favour of evil."
— Anthony Cronin

Flann died on April Fool's of a tumour lodged
    at the back of his nose
like something of life he'd caught wind of early
but congealed, then, to a solid, though mistaken,
    notion of fixity.
On the Dun Laoghaire-to-Holyhead boat I'd wept
    in the throes
of hilarity — the wintering mice of K's toes
nesting under my bum — could've been weeping
    for the Irish Sea,
its crinkled, jade glumness and ratchety Geiger
    activity,
for all the bearded Americans seated two rows
over knew. They were having a go, a cappella, at
    The Who's
"I Can See for Miles" which, recasting this now, I can
see I should've joined in on. The present is always
    misspent.
At Swim was a slog through Gaelic, gags and
    Finn McCool,
but the Kafka-on-laughing-gas of *The Third Policeman*
truly won me. Though it drowned, later, in a puddle at our
    tent's low end.

Thingymajig

The friend of a friend of mine commissioned — if
you can call it that, where twenty
bucks and Lou Reed's

Berlin stand in as payment — from a friend
of his who worked in machine
shops a custom-

welded foraging tool he put to good work Jacques
Cousteauing through the leagues of cast
offs, discards, used-ups,

and general rot that poured daily into urban Dumpsters,
bearing him ass-up, aloft, down alleyways
like a well-engineered

system of locks. We hear he's prospering. That low-end
Canadarm practically prosthesis now,
enabling the acquisitionally

challenged to dive in head first. So, one of these, then;
a soldered something they only made one
of, an imagined gadget

no one should be without that reaches corners we can't
and serves as counterweight to Bishop's "Art
of losing isn't hard

to master." Finding what it is we lost, want, or most need's a tougher
nut, but valuing the devalued might
get me it faster.

Gull

Wedge of compressed smog,
a muscled cloud-arrow fitted
with sirens in place of a head;
that tattered no-note pitched
at pure dissonance. Evolution
pissed off. Right leg lost
at the knee, chewed, a dead-root nub,
but bored numb at that, unmoved.
The short straw drawn and
shirked off. Matted ruff of scum
from the throat to an anus
that can't quit. Spits in derision
at an ungiving gutter. From the side
of its head spots one nugget of gunk
aswim in a puddle's blue oil and pistons
a hinged clamp to swallow it whole
then swivels its vision —
that core-sample of coal —
to find itself in a fun house, fifty
different versions of need to compete with.

Marsh Theatre

Reeds like violin bows quiver in the pit, glinting
in low, angled light. They point to grey
weather, an incoming chill curdling beyond
the porticoes of stripped willow.
A thousand exclamation marks in dun-coloured
felt are skewered on wands, on flagpoles driven
into the murk, where NASA turtles
mime zero-gravity walk, knocking
up silt clouds that roll like mushrooms
of cream in black tea. Walnut skulls adrift
in a dark they've yawned into being —
a backstage of jostle and bump and *so what*,
a barbiturate calm in the brain stem —
blinking leather change-purse lids, wondering
at nothing but what it might be to wonder.
A frigid gel cataracts the one floodlight.
Their sky freezes solid; a stage, a mirror in front
of which they suck in arrogant underbites, hook
horned thumbs into waistcoat folds and
audition for the only role going: stone —
stone for a run of months,
to mild applause from mallards who missed
a cue, who stand and sit down and stand and
sit down. Delicate ankles shackled in the cold snap.

Regenerative

That dog padded home wearing a rip
in his back, clicked onto the kitchen linoleum
with a five-inch smile down his saddling spine.

Where pebbles and dark grit stuck to the wound's
lips, vertebrae like molars grinned through
in an anemic bluish white. The dumb grey

meat of his tongue like a sodden flag waiting
for breeze in the post-storm still of that house —
how he lashed the plucked chicken length of it,

then lapped at the seepage that hung from black
flews. He turned, and turned, and in turning sparks
of shock shot from his eyes as his chances of seeing

pain dimmed, coiled to a brute whine in his chest. I
pictured a bald nest of lab mice pulsing in there
crying its cancer away; pictured a shed door, askew

on its hinges, mowing thick weeds as it swung; even
pictured a field in that dog, where choirs of crickets
sawed through the night with the ache in their legs.

I could smell the top-heavy cattails' thinning brown
felt as it burst, breathing commas on parachutes
into the world; heard the travelling s's of garter snakes

playing wet grass blades with cadmium scales as
they passed through invisible shivers. A lost leather
sneaker shone near a stump, like a child's plug-in

night-light, or a chipped-off sample of moon. Blue
shell casings coughed funnelled web from the throats
where their packed shot had been, and bleached-out

pages of porn doubled as mainsails, fitted to masts
of wild rose. Dew, meltwater cold, slid down my calves
like wet wrists unburdening jewels in my boots. Then no one

I knew approached through the dark, swinging a carved
column of light, prodding the bramble and weeds with
this staff that worked like a blind man's stick in reverse.

The mauve starbursts of thistles passed through it, casting
peaked shadows like crowns. Bugs strafed the beam, reared
from the black, threading it again, and again. He didn't

call out or raise his free hand or even target his lamp
on my head, just kept cresting the weeds with the twin
prows of his knees while scanning the foreground

for snags. Whether it was that he couldn't imagine me
there, and therefore I wasn't, or that my body actually
weighed in at nothing, doused as it was in that field's

feral moulting, bucking, breathing — its bull-stubborn
morphing of intrauterine moments — I couldn't decide.
There wasn't time. He passed on the left, dragged by

his light as if some shadowy, leashed mastiff tractored
him on, plunging through weed. Solid black silhouette, receding,
until distance undermined outline, form bled into field.

Public Space

Wandering wordless through the heat of High
Park. High summer. Counting the chipmunks
who pause and demand the scrub stand by
till their flitty, piggybacked equal signs can think
through this math of dogwood, oak whip, mulch.
Children glue mouths to ice cream and chips, punch
and kick at the geese, while rug-thick islands
of milt-like scum sail the duck pond's copper stillness —
Over-fat, hammerhead carp with predator brains . . .
        We can wreck a day on the shoals of ourselves.
Cramped, you broke last night and wept at the war,
at the ionized, cobalt glow that fish-tanked the air.
We're here to be emptied under the emptying sky,
eyes cast outward, trolling for the extraordinary.

To Willow

1.
Your sorrow —
        feelers, antennae —
                your sorrow.

2.
In winter's throat, this light like a grey film of greyer film
from the thirties, there's that much smoke: a great rigging
of cloud stalled in doldrums like a drugged armada,
the plume from the pipe where the dryer's at work
and my own exhaling and the dog exhaling and
every chimney visible from this suburban breezeway —

3.
I'm out of work. Willow, I'm broke.

4.
One arrives at a bad time yet wants, simply, to be,

5.
meaning during any nut shortage each spiral
of squirrel inside you spirals tighter, stays
out of it longer, tugging the quilted dark in
its fingers, gnawing on nothing, dreaming
plenitude with its teeth.

6.
Every D string ever snapped
by Joe Strummer. Marcus
Aurelius growing his hair out.
René Lévesque's lung in negative,
or that unforgettable comb-over,
again, and again, and again . . .

7.

How one day last week a Cooper's hawk lit in a low elbow
of yours, a thick crook only feet from the earth, and it gripped
in its talon what looked like a pigeon, the soft boneless flop
of its form onto bark, its near-weightless skull striking wood
like a mid-range xylophone note. Its black eye a full stop
in a language all verb.

8.

The feeding.
And in the eaves other pigeons rehearsing short speeches, sounding
vaguely impressed.

The drama
you're centre stage for, the drama you're the black backdrop for,
and the drama you watch.

9.

I remember as a child each spring being ordered
to stay clear of the mudflats and each spring
venturing down to those mudflats where the river
had bloated, flooded the trunks of six willows,
then receded again to a manageable brown gush.
Drawn by the deep sucking pits each step left
behind as we struggled — the flatulent, choked
mud, its stink of rain-barrel bottoms, of hot
attic wood — we couldn't resist, and our goal was
the willows: to grab three or four wind-braided
lifelines then watch ourselves sink waiting for help.

10.

Hearing: *find me*

>*find me*

>>*don't find me.*

11.

How your insistent, years-long stooping could
be taken for the weight and waiting
that will come with age; that downcast
gaze toward comforts cradled
in seed, but as easily seen
as disposition. Strategy of flux. Thin
whips of unhurried reach, like the makeshift
fishing rods that allowed us brown-rivered
afternoons filled with confronting
precisely nothing,
and all that nothing had to teach.

Another Dim Boy Claps

The first book you truly
understood
sent your days into

flatspin. Indiscretions,
indirection, applauding
it all glumly, bending

whatever soft metal
those chicken arms
could bend. Landing

at Mirabel from Shannon
you found the plateau
a throng of jugglers,

no one you knew answered
their phone, Hell's Kitchen
shut with a *whumpf*,

lifting litter into
the traffic. Your thumb
went up, a letter box

flag, and we sank
back into the valley.
Men drilled into cutaways

in the roadside, planted
charges and it rained
granite over the rail line.

Women acquired labs in
German cities, their language
bladed, distant as the pole-

star. You shrugged off every
option that wasn't
a long wait in a dim room

for who knew what. You
played the larval card while
they tightened their belts

and stood up to the days:
softball, CorningWare, baptisms.
You wanted a lot less than

the albatross of never
having loved. The seasons
did what they do and you

quit feigning an interest;
some roads widened, big
constrictor snakes with a fawn

lodged in their gullets. There
were some successes. But mostly
you maundered past ballparks

in the meaty evenings,
deciding to live, checking
the feeling that followed

against the length and depth
of the backstop's shadow.

To Only Occasionally Ever Actually Look

I could see it through the bus window, hovering in the changed light
over the field that was on its way into the space we had just come

through, the time we had recently abandoned, and it pointed its eyes
down at the small occurrences that happen so close to the earth, on

its surface, in fact, without fanfare. Then it was gone; not because —
or not only because — of my seat on the bus being shuddered and

thrown into the distance ahead, but due more to its suddenly folding,
collapsing to a constricted, streamlined version of itself that plunged

into the high grass as if into an ocean. There was a yellow front-end
loader unmanned on hills of parched-looking gravel, and trees

bordering the field, being waltzed with by wind. There were power
lines. It meant something to have watched it disappear, to have lost

it in the violence it chose to veil in a sargasso of wildflower and weed.
It had braved a path in spite of. Had starred in the theatre of its dream

without pause or regard for the hung jury we glance down perishing
minutes disguised as.

City Square, Giacometti

And he knew on a Tuesday there was no city but him, no neighbour,
    stranger, or mother with pram but
his bronze skull and the iron of him. Under poplar and street signs,
    there was the pinched, thumbed-on
iron of him and the iron of them; fastened and fast-disappearing
    and headed away. His worry was contour
extending outward for miles, backward for decades, inward for
    countless units of measure he'd no slide
rule but song with which to tally. It was the bending back into blue
    of high right angles; was the texture
of tree bark like moon rock, and seedpods collected at curbside
    alongside wrappers, pen lids, packet foil;
was the bubble and warp of fifteen layers of paint and his saying
    "fifteen layers of paint" aloud to cover
the ache rivering down from where his tongue was sewn on through
    to his ankles' rivets. It was him in a fixed
trajectory but spinning and shrinking while a starling looked on,
    the concrete abutment looked on. A dog,
sheet glass, orange haze, plumbing, doughnuts in display cases,
    chinstraps, cobble-stone, rocket juniper
looked on but stayed upright and offset his dry retching of place
    welded in place.

The Off Chance

Come back into the world, little twinge,
        random gesture. We've watched
    you captain the tail

of a house cat, saying the compulsion to move,
        to displace even a fraction
    of the sea of what is,

need not be linked to equation or rooted in cause.
        Let us wave to what's
    leaving in ease.

Come back constant hum of home; akin
        to what seeps gently into the sternum
    from the hanging lamps

along wet streets past midnight,
        but is cast on a frequency not fitting
    our ears. Goldenrod growing

upward on a freeway's embankment;
        the core keeping the cormorant still,
    watching the waves in their

endlessness. Whatever drone in the centre
        that lullabies, calms a pine cone
    till it unbinds its scales in the breeze,

lullabies also the earwig, urchin, oak, toad.
        Us in the pitch of our storms.

Come back not just liveable moment but
        moment of hospice; you of the malleable
    limit, of the illusory edge,

where our feet, throats, thoraxes, scalps, spines
        aren't discarded
     but grown into, while the things

of the world continue perfectly resembling
        themselves in their oddness,
     and any other bright variant

we might pull out of the toy box: sand in the cement's cracks;
        a snow slope
     in the Pyrenees. Unripened pear

on the windowsill; a fossilized tear
   left over from something's extinction.

Humber Trail Pastoral

In the eye of a milder storm off the sewage
plant, we paused on the path, looking
into the tea-coloured river at a starburst
of minnows, a moving model
of sperm head-butting the floating ovum of a bread crust.
On this bank, a man fishing snagged
and began conducting — the far shore's
foliage, metal-glint sparrows in flight,
gnats in the tree shade — to a rising
crescendo nobody heard.
                              A child, deep
in the reeds, found a shoe and a mattress and seemed pleased.
The branches, sifting the light, bristled
in an orgy of larvae that dripped. Wild
chicory and brown empties bowed their heads at an old fire
pit, while a night heron on deadwood
stalked nothing forever.
                              Before coming
across that snake near the picked-cleaned skull of a muskrat

I wanted the things I saw to appear as they'd been intended,

to see myself in the settings, even off to the left, but proportional,

the way one can look into a landscape and feel needed, compositionally

rooted, turning away, reclining in the chilled ultraviolet —

Not this panic of change, of things shedding the skin of themselves

to emerge into each moment as versions of things, still stitched to their shadows, and gaping, and blind. No arrangement felt true

enough to be held, to be fixed in memory for a time when I wasn't —

So I married myself to fair guesses, maintained a safe distance

from you and watched, and walked on like a man with a future.

Given Favourable Conditions

You believed they would return, years on. People — their pressure
and presence — would seek you out through the grain of some
    Wednesday's
gravid weather, find you busy but pensive, muttering into a green

duffle pregnant with laundry. By letter, long flight, or their own
secondhand hatchback, you kept in mind their returning, their slip
and latch into a clean socket, one of the waited-on parts

to the engine you'd made your life into. You pictured their peaceful
return and revival as if lives were like fads or seasons and gained
something precious through years of neglect: an intimate, sayable

knowledge of the planed-down, weathered oak plank that is your soul
from their perspective. Between them and you grew up highways, silos,
bad decisions, holidays, forest fires, firings and quittings: you thought

these a safe buffer, believing they would return. Family, fissured
and dissolved decades past, and irreplaceable friends whose love
you hadn't the mettle to stand foursquare and tend to. You

pictured a time when trees, brickwork, bridges had settled, finally,
into the somehow holy, into the intricate, star-sewn fabric
of themselves that had until now always hung rucked, a torque

at the seams, gathered, pinched as though each thing on earth were
some agitated angel in the weather's ill will. A time when your own
    courage to act,
to set right the flaws, would flow coterminous to their blood's

unease at absence. You'll have acquired, by attrition, these vitals
    of spirit
during a stripped-down sojourn in Glasgow, Nepal, or Berlin,
    you'll have
grown porous, a beggar, cored as you are now by this kestrel's keen

wing-stab in takeoff — an algebra'd beauty that travels via
    the budding,
x-rayed lung of a maple splayed out before you, spreading its
    dark lace
work of shadow like vipers on the lawn the lawn will swallow —

Conditions

Or it wasn't *people* who left you wading this frigid
separateness, though loss might be parsed as such and
their addresses, scribbled in a workbook's back pages,

seem one poured-over formula for reaching elsewhere's
essence. Wrongheaded. This jay, though, bobbing into pooled
water where the garden tap leaks, English china blue-white

of its wings and tail, or talons palsied round power line
where it crosses the trellis like brittled grey rag-coils of last
season's grapevine; unhaunted cock of its head looking up, back,

behind, *through* you to where the lime sheen of three fruit flies
confabbing on warm porch wood completes a dizziness, an abundance
of goings-on that have vowed to be piercingly not you. Obstinate

unlikeness: the hornet's wing a maple key that never was
    a hornet's wing.
Or how you stared at a plate-load of skeleton — sticklebacks grilled
with garlic and lemon — as conversation dolphined up from a lull,
    grinned,

then plunged back into the ring of drunk friends leaving you
tranced still, stuck in that pile of charred Cyrillics, or scintilla, maybe,
of an ongoing feast offered to Tacitus. Fish with its mouth stitched

shut. We never come round from this coma of looking.

Late Reading

Penniless, late August night, poor light over
milkish boardwalk slats. A broad bank
of tire-rubber-grey cloud blots not
quite all of the moon, so vast sheet-
metals of gin-bottle aquamarine slice
through what's here:

                   a wing-tucked swan
in the wedge of its tree root, the tattooed
chest of a park bench, feet screwed down tight,
that languorous owl's hoot spelled out with
wreaths around a wrought-iron war
memorial's base. On the beach, facing
the breakwater, this solitary high chair
backlit by the moon strikes me as vaguely
Greek. More so when I make out the sign:
OF DUTY —

            Civic? Familial? Under
God? I should detach, climb the six
rungs, perch in the chair, and watch —
patient, paced — unreadable happenings
happen to an alchemical sky, its metallic
purples melt, diffuse, quartz splinters
smother, blink out, some other, warmer,
less unending hue approach from the lake,
ascend the same ladder and join me there,
newly vigilant over no
life on earth. I should, it's late.

As You Were

Owl in the elm. You can feel it. Listening a sieve no moving

      thing slips through. Warm,

well-lit room. The window's a mirror, behind which the city slackens,

      softens; noise distinguished from noise but all shut

           into shadow. There's nowhere to go at this hour.

Like rafts of rough blowdown — burdens soaked in — we

      drift, snag, and drift in the bland, seamless

           river of days. Luggaged with notions of how

childhood passed as simple, detached, time without weight —

           That factory yard and littered

low brush beyond, mapped and strong-armed by the unwitnessed

unguessing imaginations of kids: the asphalt an airstrip,

the hedges and bramble, jungle or forest; weedy, rust-caked twists

      of machinery were burned-out

remains of heavy artillery. And the wood platform spiked into

      an ash, our surveillance post, sniper roost, and H.Q.

The factory remained. Remained and sprawled, like a cinder-block

chaperone, staring out from its rows of smashed eyes —

but when a prisoner was bound to the loading

dock rails, the scavenged ropes used were real and

unreal, his pleading heard and not, heeded

and not. Disquieting to think, now, of him being grilled,

arm-burned, or worse, for information he

could ever have only made up on the spot. His interrogators left

to decide (scratching naked knees, brushing

off pangs from a skipped dinner) whether this or that cooked-up

kid's plot was sufficiently true.

Answers offered now are as groundless. The grilling, softer:

How have I lived? Am I to become

what I think of myself? Will the world meet

and embrace me halfway, like a child chased

out of some skeletal night park into his own

arms, startled?

Only so many sounds the night will admit. Aching,

caged drone of traffic far off, small lippy

consonants deep in the plumbing, pliant complaint

from an arthritic chair leg, and the owl; memory,

its pulled-out, full-throated *o*'s

that loop these nights, then tighten.

Drinker

Foot. Foot. Each step a flat, thankless event
undoing itself, or threatening to, like slapping
wet beach sand —

some squat shorebird's legs, loose-hinged,
their ballasted ankles flinging: progress
of the grinning

maimed. Even the chin squashed onto a bellows
chest and deadweight, obtuse-angled elbows
is pure oil-

slick cormorant. Soft, soft cement. Every shut but
still blue-lit shop's interior's as good as a bed.
Pints plinthed up

from belly to head and that black, fearful, wobbling
blot now studied down the slope of the nose, spoken to:
"A roti'd be

magic." And answered when it asks its own name: "You?
You're an ousted, excised, exiled form of panic" —

Morning

If anything like mercy had the controls,
        the sun would switch off. Shakes
                in the marrow, in a bodhran-heart. I'm

done. Rook-noise borne in on long moans
        off the street. Be still in your swamp.
                Nerve-ends a garden rake through

the burnt lawn of the sheet. All
        psalms gone, again child again
                born into the neglect of a world

that won't pay out into you Welcome.
        Self-sorry and sweating. Only a smidgen
                left of unused inner space. Slip

chance in — very nearly said *grace*.

The Painting on the Cover of *Otherwise*

A small pond dug
into a footpath that bisects
a French garden. The neat
hedgerows bend, obey.

There must be wind. Clay
so clean, so reddened in
the light, our eye rakes it
for bits of litter, heel-scuffs,

a sparrow, anything —
What sort of people design such order,

and who tends it? Is this heaven?
Or is peace that almond haze where

hard edges slip glimpsed through
the doorless gate, the unclipped
immaculate beyond the vined
wall that darkens the middle distance?

Prayer

A day in the country is over, now shuffles its parts
like playing cards, dropping some, creasing
the corners of others, ruining them.
                                        I am far
from sleep, so abandon the house for moonlight;
for a sensory pocket — that broadened meanwhile
in love with death — where what's recently gone's
more there than what's there.

                                Here are impressions
in the Queen Anne's lace and Indian grass where
some of them rested or fell. The light silvers the edges,
darkens the centre. I hold my own hand and wait.
A hobo's weathered bundle hangs and hums —
papery eye, layered eye that can stare you into fits —
a tenor drone dividing night, dissolving through the sumac.

My friends, gentle, unknowable to me, wrapped
in exquisite quilts, haul tomorrow down upon us,
we're that much farther from the start.

Unseasonable Warmth

Paused in the shadow of bereavement, in the long shadow behind
a rooftop billboard at the terminal end of Queen St. West, under

the latticed and scaffolded backside; some crude transistor panel,
its soldered nodules of starlings clustered in the matrix. Pulling a hand

from the weathered dories of quartered melons beached in a shop
stall, you've tagged a cluttered longing that paws at the given, shirks,

recoils far short of clarity. O ineffectual mouth, admit to loving the world
to bits
        and pieces . . .
              Saying, "What can I know?" — "Do not presume, one
of the thieves" — "You can't take it with you" — "How should I begin?"
All that.
              Scene: you're tottery, leaning in the living ellipsis, swamped
in the world's brute demand that it resemble itself. Loss won't be thought

through. Likenings abound, abide. Sun-glint buttering the corrugated
lake. Gilt causeway could carry you to Buffalo.
                  A face clouding over,
the lake's crust peels back, loosening a pool where geese are preening
clipped wings, honking at transports that bull down the off-ramp,

long necks like middle fingers gloved in black kid, or spigots tapping
the lake's music, or garden stakes driven in to support whatever shoots
up after the flooding recedes . . .

           Eyes down, touch your toque and go.

Lords of the Little Gestures

His Life as Apprentice out West

Became a bogland of Faber and Faber books,
reading rainbows of Brits when not fitting the doors of the rich with
    new locks,
so vanished like weather into the Prairies
inching east over scrub grass and days.
Even found, north of Superior, just where it was *Brownlee*
went (down Brownlee side road bisecting the highway
petering out on a rock-jawed
spit watched over by loons)
but no way of contacting Muldoon.

His time of being barely an "I" lost in others' work now past,
he resurfaces, cogent commiserant, amid the brown brick of the east . . .
was last seen scratching his head
over a job application for a part-time position (very)
as a page in a library.

His Perilous Greyness Through Michigan

Discoloured pines, their hair combed back by the vacuum of traffic.
Crow, crow. The fossilized eggs of propane
tanks and a pizza of pheasant straddling a black
tire burn. Dowagiac. Battle Creek. Rain —
"That dream of the shark in shallow water and the view from the
        promontory and all the kiddies going under has really set my
        teeth on edge."
"We should've, maybe, eased up, hey,
on the third day?"

And so rolled both down the 94's anxiety toward a frowning
        Ambassador Bridge.

Dear cardinal, dear sore spot on the Iowan sky
inhaling your whistle — he feels he could die
for want of attachment to any one thing yet imparts
to others a sense of ease, inclusiveness, while the centre hurts,
        whistles like a wind tunnel, and hurts.
If Detroit
doesn't get him it'll be what rubbed out his Uncle Dwight.

Where His Bike Went

To Bikeland black market. To Slaveland.
2777648 sanded down to just 8.
Its stripped frame a Chinese ideogram;
unreadable, unridable. Both sprockets now paperweights.
Wide rims rigged onto some decades-old Peugeot
racing number, giving the effect of a frightened whippet
with swollen paws. *Where the hell was the law?!*
Dunno.

On foot . . . on foot . . . bereft
of his gate to the world,
he looks off to his slow, slow left
where once a maelstrom of traffic swirled,
and sees a family two-wheeler. Unlocked. The luck of it!
Hesitates, then makes off with the baby bucket.

He and He Frisbee

Mirrored huddles of older men bowled
bocce at opposite, identical squat and cracking brogues.
So serious! Stooped, smoking and howled
when their spheres clacked awry; their little rogue
stars. They were squads of Galileos
in slacks and cloth caps: good, at play,
curious. Someone's cocker spaniel looked a gross comet
bounding spastic with spitty teeth. Bright, bright workable day.
A park. A friend at the far end —
I Frisbee you you Frisbee
me. "No, dummy, it won't glow till the sun has set."
Kinematics and body mechanics do away with intent: bend,
flick, and it floats — *Don't catch it,*

don't.

It's unearthly —
The god his pleading mimicked plunged deeper in debt.

He Speaks, I Think, on Behalf of Every

Winterhorse. Oh heavy neck, help me out-exit my
head; its *doo da* (pause:) *doo da*. Created languageless, verbless —
utterly — still blow you, though, any
number of soft, heated, mushrooming exhales of Equus.

Snow is blank-faced and still with clean pleasure at
knowing, so thoroughly, Horse: can't help grinning its millionteeth.
One drift, shaped like Finland, I once saw in Westmeath,
wore a near-perfect shadow of Horse like an elongated hat

or an occupying power. As if, maybe, Hel-
sinki needed — depended, even — on . . . *What the?!*   All bull.
Hiked we once to a glacier through fair layers of packed
and unpacked early winter snow, and encrypting those undisturbed
      stretches
were meanderful small-something tracks that might've spelled Gnome
      On Crutches . . .
but didn't. And we accepted that, with very little hesitation, as fact.

His Domestic Pleasures Song

Flash-fried perogies. Wink. Antonioni.
Kurosawa. Cryptic crosswords. Kimchee.
Nights of Cabiria, Roma, Amarcord.
Out of the blue, your bathrobe doing its best Red
Sea, of its own accord. Finger paints.
Borage flowers fossilized in the ice tray.
At the business end of *War and Peace,*
getting the condensed version, in a glance.
Cat puke. Haircuts. *The Verve Collection.*
Muffins before the bananas rot. A rooftop garden.
Private language for misery, nothingness, joy,
acrimony. A list of names for a boy.
Coached to notice when mock orange is in bloom.
Left alone. But breath-sounds from the other room.

He Propositions the Toilet

Admittedly, there are other ways to laugh
but drink seemed most civil; we three become
locks happily transporting my buoyant half
to wherever might be thought of as home.

I see you still have the ring.
And I still the glue of the holding
of the fitted of the hinged
self that manages cutlery and appointments: that binged.

Odd, I was in this position when last
I prayed . . . How many years? . . . since that first
Atlantic squall ripped off the mast
and my deck's heaped rigging dreamed of the hull with thirst.
So that's really the offer: You keep the ring, I learn from you undertow.
Don't answer now, just wink as I leave so I'll know.

Winter

You can't end with nihilists.
It's too stormy and strident.

Nor can you plug this sucking chest wound with your fist —
open palm . . . steady pressure till the lung is spent.
So, OK.   And you wander away
noticing how the ambulance strobes play
with your sense of perspective,
and sirens become silence unzipping: alive.

Home. Kitchen light's woolly, weak. The sink's another wreckage
and Mum calls, stringing together
six clichés and one old adage —
like that, *adij* — barely space enough between her
d and *g* to remember you forgot to mail that letter.
Again. And Moscow is so far.

He Considers Nihilism from Inside a Culvert

Long have I dreamed! My own two suns . . .
light enough to read by, and here, agriculture
in the piddle running over ruts in this corrugated iron.

"We assent to impulse, yet impulse is bedded in NATURE!" *Nature,*
    nature
(or some such). A natural slouch. Rain-laden ditch reeds.
A natural recoil and quickness to give
in to the agoraphobe in a claustrophobe's clothes.
Free market creeds.
Obligations of love.
Just witnessing others tackling living in droves,
as if they'd arrived clear-purposed and burning,
stirs up the fears and a general yearning
for rewind to a state of inaction, or
forward to when all action is —
                    mossy gurgle, the ping of drips. Static flesh, and an echo.

Filament

"Die kiwi-seeds in mein kaki
sehen aus wie Zeken, oder Raps."
— Johannes Stender, 3½. So what caps
that?!   Tricky
little skin-flap keying a throw switch in the pharynx of the mind
   of the I in the world.

Her hair was nighttime, (while he, into its socket, installed
a love for the in flux, the blue days, the stone-chucked-into-the-divine-
   as-calm-water: then went
big with the filament)
or her hair. Like like like. Wow.

If You have willed that our heavendownhere act the ornery cow,
then our love is free
to make it up as we go. This I — check *him* out — decree.
Ottawa, Skeena, Oder, Liffey, Volga: extant
copies of the One Verse, imperfect to begin with. He wants to be 3.

Not Lonely, Ottawa-so, and Bent

Then after the bender, pushing authors
at each other's
hands; they quake, the fingers, but take to the page like tongues of cats
pointing at milk's middle;
a functional surrogate for long chats,
dialogue, mano-a-mano; read this read this read this read the pedal
on my bike is loose —

He thinks here of formative years, sees them as steps following the
    lead of a long oak banister. They're silent, formally so, silent, set
    back, shallow and disappearing into the dark heaven of a silent
    house,

formally so. I'll get her this bracelet. Crushed stone
inlay around a tulip stamped into shell of abalone.
And the light nodes pinging off the Rideau Canal
can all
be read as the better book, the wider, larger, warmer glory
of being, inside, attentive, OK, and on one's own. He's sorry.

It Unhands Him; and Sanderlings

Unhands him and drifts off, lifts, in the least a diminishment —
so that the plenary forms arrayed there always now narrowed peace
to a needle. He wept? Fine; limn the warm, pliant,
wet edge of the world. It's price
was low. Considering . . .

And sanderlings,
tiny chain gang of nervousness, compulsives kissing the million
    crustaceans, kissing themselves reflected in the silvering wash.
Clam flats. Small eels are elvers.   He liked her lonely in the salt marsh,
"Show me asters."
But she'd fixed on the folds, the crimped bracelets of light
    on the water's
wrists and wouldn't let go, "I told myself to care
where I stepped, not to slip and die quietly out here."

Rowing that punt popped an oarlock,
and a day hence prayer came, scraping: o beneficence. It gave her
    a rusted nail — it'll work.

(*He can't leave her* —
Evening, love sent a seam down the sky, his bay mauved over.)

Pietà with Breeze and a District

And so he then — in the riven gleam that gave lampposts and post-
    boxes their faces, their blackened
reverse-sides' crimped shadows rippling away over snow,
    climbing the lettered panes and
awnings of shop fronts like winter versions of vines, or damp
    in the brick, alongside fish
merchants whose chest aprons' waxed leather stank and shone,
    who drove dish-gloved arms into blue
cisterns of carp between bouquets of horse-sized steaming
    carnations that clouded the expressions
carving their faces and in the next moment gave way to new
    failures of permanence: home
and that house's goat leash, porch-lit exterior, and brain
    of moths, the pasture of *terra*
cognita from stone lintel to garden spike, without guidance,
    decorum, intent, or any
hold on north, within the boredom of errand fulfilled
    over and over and the tow-cart's
wheel a wobbling guide to humility, or proof that mechanical
    time is a joyless concoction, in
the drift near an oak door's brute weight, smelling
    the brine of Mitteleurope,
by no cleric's directive — fell, crying, intoning, *I will*.

Signal Hill

England sent *tap tap*
and *tap tap tap*, and the hill
answered back.

There were cannons
in bunkers, mines in the narrows,
the Will to Power

periscoping up
in the harbour. Those battlements
rust and whistle

there still, but splashes
of spray paint lighten the gloom,
and will for a while

if we let the vandals
roam, confettiing the concrete
with condoms, trading

in pills that alter
their vista through the gun slits
of history. The vandals

are young and make
use of the ruins. Stand back.
Thank them for that.

Lines Toward a Strategy for Travel

Who isn't dog-tired and wishing it over
five hours east of Kenora? Superior —
a cantankerous ocean where no
ocean should be, or a dumb uncle's
beer-gut stretching that belt of highway
to its last possible punched-out notch.

Ill-lit clusters of roadside cabins:
Pleasantview, Pineview, The Sleepy Hunter,
the tagged and numbered key in your cold
left hand, crunching snow underfoot en route
to our room while I docked
the van's bulk in a drift.

Brown short shag, a phone with directions,
two mummified cups, and a quilt-covered
double like a proscenium stage under its arch
of wall-mounted mallards in takeoff.
Framed in the window, the moon, like the dinged
blade of a sickle hanging unused in the tar-dark

must of a shed. There
and there, nail holes where the light tweaks
in. But what to make of him, the owner, sawing
a shot moose into freezer-sized slabs back
in that eye-splitting halogen light of the office?

"It was shot on my land, I was given a third."

Exhausted, we slid plastic over
the counter, eyeing the lost Pollock
in red on his butcher's apron, the guest
book list of visiting marksmen a lament
or prayer-wail: *Ohio, Ohio, Minnesota, Ohio* . . .

Away from here, unheard, a stunned,
scoured-out shadow of Moose bears
its top-heavy echo of shag and girth
through blue, intimate
forests of snow. Weightless. Confused.

Clothespins

In use, ties on a rail line skirting
    the sky that's a bay
        on a map.

Alone, a squid in profile
    by Picasso or Braque.

Disassembled, shrapnel
    from Juno and a whittled
        Madonna in halves.

Two back to back, a *W*
    collapsing or an *M*
        with a hat.

Thrown in the fire, just
    wire — red hot. Or stood
        on end, a tango,

a waltz, an intimate chat.
    With an eye up to
        the helix-hole,

a locket-sized portrait
    of whatever one wishes,
        living's live-action cameo —

Speed Blues Junket into Harmonica

A face cast up where metal birds ignite.
O hang this neck with penance, with retreat,
                  that we not start fights.

*[Harmonica. Harmonica as argument over last morsel. As swayback
mare. As medical chart. Weather
fronts exhaust themselves peeling away over
Harmonica. Harmonica
grifts, braggadocio, then with its graven plastic head kicked
in. Stove stoked by Harmonica
breeds left-behindness, sends a postcard.]*

             ————

He ate up all her chicken, wine, and rice
without her knowing, pinched it from its place.
                  He wasn't to her nice.

*[Harmonica as stand-in for long shot at Gethsemane. As long-
since uncut forelocks. Threshing
machines mowing in tandem four abreast shave
Harmonica before going
out. Harmonica gives Hiss kiss on temple settling into its own
UnderIce. As picked bluebell, pines
away. Harmonica pouring out tall stacks yellowish.]*

             ————

Whatever strife there was to begin with's now double.
He thinks his manservant, practical, worthy, able,
               but, Lord, unbearable.

*[Harmonica grey-beard. Calabri-Yau hoards Harmonica's seven
dimensions. Tendering resignation
Harmonica sugars the gas tank. As holdup. As*

language-death stalking the brain
base kitten-blind. Nobody touch Harmonica. As a long wait for no one.
As watercress. As not what you ordered.
Harmonica's thoroughness a tracheotomy in a tool shed.]

———

Lament lament lament lament lament.
It goes this way until ere long it's *went* —
and where his interment?

[*As timepiece, melting sundial. As thought emergent. Cannibal*
Harmonica flings hooks last-ditch
Harmonica into the elusive meat of a moment trying
to shore up the flood of what's
going. As the stringed seam of a bean. Harmonica stray-dogs about
town. Footprints Harmonica in fresh
snow, there they go. Harmonica admits to there being
not one answer. As too many.]

The Sling of Two Arms

I held her not well, didn't
      hold her well, jumped
my gaze from one eye to her other,
      seeing neither, pinned one
deadwood arm that numbed, then
      fell. I held her unwell.

The veneer headboard bent, wavered,
      its false grain a-swim like
the clean code on a wave-washed
      shell. To not be present is hell —
no, to remember having been absent;
      indisputably bodily there, legs,

lungs, teeth, and all, but watching oneself
      watching oneself holding her —
and not well. She hung in the sling of two
      arms where from greed and lust and good
greed the good go down clawing, calling up
      at their own image calling into a well.

Not well I held her, yet she still I full well.

On Feeling Low, Housed and Grateful

The secondhand iron floor lamp you rewired
and scrounged up a hat for; tattered, slatting
the light. Keep and contain me, while good

me gazes back, full of buffed grace, from the polished
convexity of a hip flask. Wide, wide smile.

I bounce off that and stay in my cave.

A checkered past has proved the worst teacher
I've grumped under since that bitter Chapel Hill
alumnus in grade ten English. I try. So what's this Durex

doing in the mickey pocket of my collar-up
Camus overcoat? Who among us isn't weakened
to see even our wardrobe's a quote?

But when I crawl into the weirdly
habitable Arctic your form makes of the white duvet,
I'm naked, and naked, and not alone.

Today, the pigeon-cacked sill outside sat battered
in autumn light, hard, aslant; specks in the lintel
glinting. It all looked genuinely . . . something.

I'll quote you, in full, to all the young hopefuls
still in me, then take another loving run
at these padded walls we edged and rolled together.

A Master Narrative

Grouped, alone, we settle ourselves beside this
       boat to wait for its unmooring —
to be helped, handled, told to load our bottles,
       bread, maps, and books into our neon
packs then marched down steps that fold

       off the deck like a drawbridge
concept we know from having been kids.
       We wait, picking out hike routes
through peaks of meringue in the blue above,
       naming each after a common thing,

declare them wondrous, and why don't they affect
       us this way in town? The sun's now
only half of one, will drown in minutes and take
       the shape of things with it. Still no
movement but shadow on deck and we can't see

       below but've heard evidence enough
of absence to allow that wasp-awkward, queasy
       sense we should have left hours ago
to horn in on our drone of *Remember when?* and
       I should've, then . . .
                   But who here would we

ask? Why — fitted out as we are and late for nothing
       as nothing awaits us — get tense? A moored
boat will creak and rub the night to day, or until some
       drunk appears in the slicker and cap
I picture him in to make light work of these bristling

       pig's brains of damp knots and cast off.
The water's coming in or going out. Lapping, boiling,
       it cups mossed pilings underneath
the dock, sounding like the need-to-know phrases
       in the language of the place we came

here headed for. I've only sounded them out as they
           undressed themselves to my untrained
ear in the Fodor's I plucked from a remainder bin,
           so I could well be confusing *The cost
of fare from here to there* with *What is your point*

           of origin? Anticipation of finally setting
out proves as exhausting as any going. Cigarette ends
           flare, arc, and fsst. One, now, slips under,
having jotted her first note home: *Am not alone. About
           to embark. Can't tell you how excited* —

and we'll follow her soon, into disjunctive, grief-struck
           dreams of never having come: the sun-
stroke, ice floe, mirror-calm page before page one.

Fall: Three Views, One Window

1. Mouse Hole

This window gives onto a windowless
brick wall where house sparrows, winged
mice, home in on holes
in the ochre exterior —
                          dappled tan blurs flitting,
fretting, howevering
over sad, stagnant hydrangeas exhaling
gnat-clouds into October's bluster.

Gangs of groundleaf riot,
                relax.
The earth's skin crawls,
so it hugs itself —
our sandals reappear healed over, suddenly boots, and
soldierly stand their position
on the collage of newsprint, having gone nowhere in days.
The storm pane casts
back our room, unpeopled, from the pre-dinner dark and
we turn from the prospect
of living in there, reach for stray things (oddments, clutter,
rind, string), grow hungry-
bored, and gnaw through the burlap rice sack, the electrical wiring.

2. Manhole

Or I put the mournful, harpy lyric away and look outside, where
what I thought was a scrap
of tar paper or blown shingle poking up from the mat of wet

leaves turns out an abandoned black docker's cap — picture a toque
but rolled up like a condom — and
it lies there, in the downpour, sucking the weather into itself with all

the finality of a full-stop ending autumn's rambling run-on sentence.
It's telling the story of a city
employee who'd been cleaning the drainage grates of the season's leaf-

slop, the now-sopping scurf bound and glued to blowdown sticks, when
he gave in to the urge he'd thought
locked away in that sheet-metal barn alongside his lunch, to leap before

looking, just as he'd done as a kid, on his own, a few times even off
the roof of the dog run. Why he's
in it now, though, up to his eyes, I shy from explaining, not being near

as adept at the ending of stories as I am at the lifting of lids off gloomy
scenarios just long enough to get
a whiff of the runoff, the runnels of subsurface flow. More the stand-

offish, dissociative type; our protagonist's boy-self, say, come upon
the crown of his own head in that
leaf mound like olives he'd picked out of salads and — bent kneed,

stooped, curled-out-over alone with his moment's unease — has turned
the dark end of the world's prose
into a — *look* — a question mark.

3. F Hole

Strung over the crosswalk, three
yellow boxes marked X: a lantern
festival in a red-light district.
They're reminders; though it never
appears so, the neighbourhood's pornographic.

A brownstone with lights
burning on the second floor.
The west window lowers its blind.
I wink back. *Je t'adore.*

A low-flying merlin, straying out of High Park,
eclipses a 747 descending into Pearson from Newark.

You, coming and going, hair snaked
down your back and tied with a ribbon.
I'm seeing the F hole in the cheap Gretsch
I owned in grade eleven; my thrashings, posings —
and point of pride, never once
attempting "Stairway to Heaven."

The same bird, about to depart for O'Hare,
gets word from air traffic control: Stay here.

Working the Lakefront

Lovely black tug, slow,
like a snowplow under streetlight or one
bumper car, unhitched, left alone
on the lake

to bash its blunt
bow at the mist. Finally, one bird that isn't
a gull silently drops like
a dart into wake.

Noon. The sky sets an
undecided, dead colour like concrete and I've heard
the reappearance of sturgeon
proves the lake is

cleaning itself. We suffer from
what is more than ourselves. This is union-wage work;
catered, bottled water in
iced coolers, time-

and-a-half, double, triple,
but every break spent here at this lake's grey edge,
"my wife —" and "next week —"
and "my beautiful

boat —" flicking spent butts
at the widening rings where the whatever-bird has
surfaced with silver in shock
in its throat.

Lyman M. Davis: Built 1873, Burned 1931

The night sky a frost spangled tarmac,
and a moon pouring its mind out over the lake. A boardwalk

soldiered on where the train line ended.
There must've been lemonade, or honeydew, and the burned

demerara of warm horse scent. Her masts creaked
amidships, moaned, but she was happy to be towed out into the ink

then doused, her rivets and bolts having run
their course, run down to threadless, leaky nubs

that popped and shot when her bulk was torched.
The flames' petals cupped her, grew, sucking in sound, perched

like an orchid afloat in the dark of a botanist's
dream. The fire writing Arabic on the eyes of a summering crowd

that grinned in the red-orange tint, saying
to no one, their neighbour, "Imagine. A volcano born in Lake Ontario."

Or offered this into the deeper funnel
of the horses' ears where it sank, bathed, resting in the steam off

their brains. Short spell of what's beautiful
submerged in a hiss: we mistake each luminous thing for another.

To See It for What It Isn't until We Have to Go

Habit that began on the Plateau, perhaps,
or letting that latch click shut past
midnight then out to squint through

the indifferent dark at an indifferent
town — ill-clothed, unintentioned. Spearing
church spires, Scotch thistle angering

the unused lots where structures stood
or fell depending on their mood. The bridge,
untended cedar hedge, blank drive-in, and

Jeeps on blocks, were as they were on prior
walks. So, habit seeded by hours soaked
in indirection, ennui, when seeing meant

seeing an object recede, like a thing one loved
that couldn't love back or even mimic the act
of attention, and so to draw it near

was to costume it in rags you'd dredged
from where the trestle's pilings stood like
customs guards and made the river give

over its holdings.
                                    Call it the tug of our
sense of being somehow less; of having
wandered so far from whatever centre

that any echo died in transit, became
the leftovers of small animals who'd called
a rough halt to it in the outlying acreage

with no hope of a watcher, praying, tying twigs
together. At night I'll imagine remembering X
pulling over where I walked along the verge,

his gleaming Dodge rumbling like the changeable
heart of the world, "It's my goddamn chariot,
get in, but puke on the seats and I'll shootcha."

Do we get a little precious about it? Yes, and why
not, if we fail to inflate the loved in order to take
in more, we're left with what it was.

Fire Watch

Hello, listen, I'm on a field phone, do not speak until I say "over."
Repeat, don't talk until I say "over." Over. Do you understand,
or is your silence intentional? Over.
Northwest of the Seven

Sisters, in a sort of bunker on stilts. Over. Last week I called in a cobra
of smoke. I was packing my gear in a panic, when
the next tower west confirmed it was only
low cloud. Over. I

get a crackling out of Alaska that sounds religious. Vladivostok. CBC.
I've decided I like Paganini. Over. No, leave it, or throw
it out, I won't need it here. If ever.
Over. When storms wander

across the lower jaw of the coastal range, unloading their cargo here,
it's like being in the engine room of something metallic
and massive. Over. My first grizzly passed
within a stone's throw,

followed an hour later by the sucking thumps of a Parks chopper.
Nothing since. Over. Days, I rearrange stones shoaled up
at the base of the uprights and struts.
Nights, I stab at imagining

anything lovely, but end up laughing. Over. The forest goes quiet as if
waiting for me to finish. Listens hard to whatever isn't
itself. Makes me anxious. I think
of how we ever came to . . .

[inaudible] given the arm's length I kept joy at. Over. Affection stung
like a rasp drawn over [inaudible]. I thinned the world of it.
Don't live as I did. Allow for terms
of relief. The black

maples aligned along streets, waddling skunks, their dark dusters
through the foxglove, your shoulder bag, shoes, the faces
of strangers; all may strike you as fibres
of a tremendous sadness.

That's you *in among the weave of it*, new. Over. Is that important?
I've been contracted to watch this horizon and will
be here until something happens. Over.
Tell them it will. Over.

Epilogue

Before the door on its seized hinge ushered in weeping,
      before postures of grief and the many tearings of veils,
when the common and wasted colluded and heaved,
      before it slid, lead-coloured, gaseous, up the throat

of its geyser, carpeting walkways, meadows, foyers,
      and wharves, before it became everywhere, before
it happened, thumb-crushing the pharynx of the continuous now,
      before lakes, before it ministered to echoes wandering

the palace corridors, before the palace itself and its plated
      imported shinings, before corvid, millstone, hymnal,
before the singing of hymns, lament's long whip
      that cracked in the eye, before train wheels, toads, burnt

navigational charts, before zero and heat, sound,
      disease, before sound, before what next?
And before what? Before waiting, lying, inhaling, killing,
      before unendurable wait, before shattered, its attendant

cavern-eyed dogs, before it without witness occurred
      on the slopes then seeped into the valley, before motion,
clothing, civics, before the shock waves of failure,
      or a goat's bleat hardening in the high air before air —

Notes

1. "Thingymajig" was written in response to a question put to the author and others by *Saturday Night* for their millennium issue: What idea, trend, or technology *should* make an impact on our lives in the next century?
2. "Another Dim Boy Claps" is after Richard Hugo's poem "The Freaks at Spurgin Road Field."
3. "*Lyman M. Davis*: Built 1873, Burned 1931" was a decommissioned lake ferry set ablaze off Sunnyside Park for amusement.

Acknowledgements

The author gratefully acknowledges the assistance of The Ontario Arts Council.

Several of the poems appeared in the following publications: *Exile, Malahat Review, Queen Street Quarterly, THIS Magazine, Saturday Night*, and the anthology *Why I Sing the Blues*. Thanks to the editors of each. Other poems were commissioned for and aired on CBC's *Out Front — Poet's Premiere*. I am indebted to my editor and friend A. F. Moritz for his essential work at the end. And to the friends — Suzanne Buffam, David O'Meara, Don McKay, Adam Sol, and Tamas Dobozy — whose genius, collective and separate, went into the making, I owe more than just thanks.